THE HISTORY OF EXPLORATION
DRAKE
& THE ELIZABETHAN EXPLORERS

New
Forest
Press

Publisher: Tim Cook
Editor: Guy Croton
Designer: Carol Davis
Production Controller: Ed Green
Production Manager: Suzy Kelly

ISBN: 978-1-84898-304-5
Library of Congress Control Number: 2010925459
Tracking number: nfp0003

U.S. publication © 2010 New Forest Press
Published in arrangement with Black Rabbit Books

PO Box 784, Mankato, MN 56002
www.newforestpress.com

Printed in the USA
9 8 7 6 5 4 3 2 1

Contents

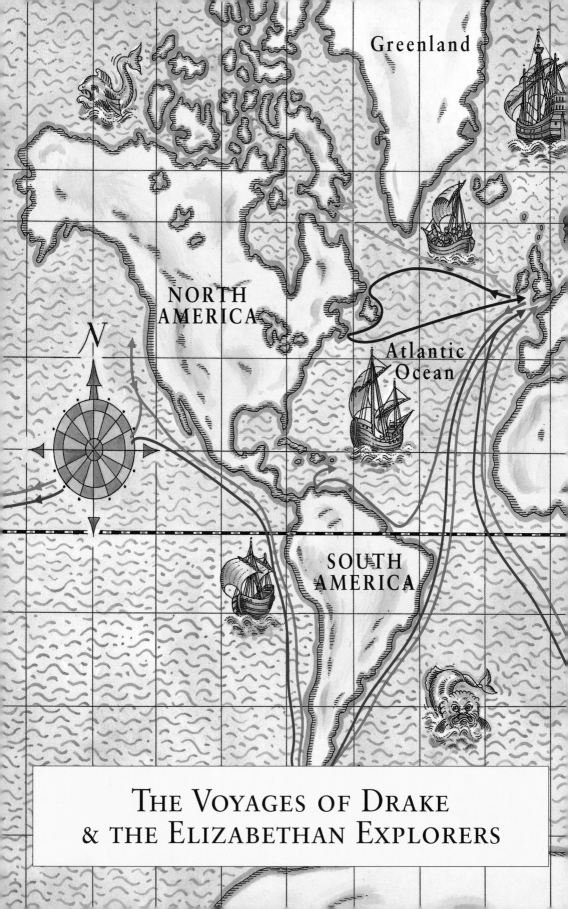

Greenland

NORTH
AMERICA

Atlantic
Ocean

SOUTH
AMERICA

N

THE VOYAGES OF DRAKE
& THE ELIZABETHAN EXPLORERS

Russia

EUROPE

China

India

AFRICA

Indian
Ocean

Australia

Antarctica

KEY

Drake
Frobisher
Cavendish
Raleigh
Cabot

DISCOVERY

Exploration, that is the discovery of new lands, peoples, and cultures, has existed as long as humankind itself. It was however, between the 1400s and 1600s during the "Age of Discovery" that exploration and discovery became increasingly important. It was the need for power and trade, especially for spices and precious metals, that drove the European explorers to seek out new trading partners and lands to colonize. Along with improvements in shipbuilding, map reading, and navigation, this was a time of great change in the European view of the world.

Since the ancient Greeks, people had believed that the Earth was at the center of the universe, with the Sun, Moon, and stars rotating around it. This was known as the Ptolemaic (or geocentric) model. This theory remained popular until the late 1500s, when it was replaced by the Copernican (or heliocentric) model, championed by Nicolaus Copernicus and later Galileo Galilei, in which the planets rotate around the Sun. The people of medieval Europe had a very different view from us about the rest of the world. They did not have the benefit of newspapers, telephones, or television, so news hardly ever reached ordinary people. Unlike today, they were not able to fly from one continent to another. In fact, very few people went farther than their nearest town during the whole of their lives. However, the way that medieval Europe looked at the world was to be changed forever by two explorers: Christopher Columbus, who sailed westward and found a new world in the Americas, and Vasco da Gama who sailed eastward and found a sea route to Asia.

CHRISTOPHER COLUMBUS

Christopher Columbus's intention was to find a westward route to China and the East Indies, as an eastward route was blocked by Muslim lands hostile to Europeans. Although Columbus was never to find Asia in his voyages, he did discover the continent of America after sailing across the Atlantic Ocean in 1492. He held the belief that it would be possible to continue sailing westward to reach Asia via America.

A VIEW OF THE WORLD

This is Ptolemy's world map, first produced in 1482. It shows how little of the world Europeans really knew about. Southern Africa, the Pacific Ocean, and the American continent are not included and Asia seems to be a matter of guesswork. Only the mapping of the Mediterranean is accurate. Even the outlines of Scotland and Ireland look strange to modern eyes.

FERDINAND MAGELLAN

Columbus' dream was to go on to inspire Ferdinand Magellan, whose voyages proved that, as Columbus believed, it was possible to reach Asia by traveling westward. Magellan traveled around South America, and across the Pacific Ocean, discovering the Strait of Magellan.

FRANCIS DRAKE

Francis Drake was to become the first Englishman to successfully circumnavigate the globe. He was commissioned by Queen Elizabeth I of England to sail across the southern Atlantic through the Strait of Magellan and to attack the Spanish treasure ships and settlements on the unprotected west coast of South America.

DRAKE—THE EARLY YEARS

The name of Sir Francis Drake is best identified with England's defeat of the Spanish Armada, his circumnavigation of the world, and with stories of heroic raids upon the Spaniards in the Caribbean. As with so many heroes, however, the story is more complex. Francis Drake was born to a humble farming family in Devon, England. He might have become a farmer himself had his father not been an outspoken Protestant lay preacher who was forced to leave his home, with his family, to seek safe refuge in Kent, England. They lived for some years on board a hulk moored on the River Medway, which no doubt fired up the imagination of the young Francis. He was apprenticed to the owner and captain of a small coaster that traded between England and the Netherlands. His distant cousin John Hawkins secured him a position as purser on a slave-trading voyage, and he soon rose to the rank of captain.

DEFENDING THE FLEET

When Drake's father arrived in Kent, he became a lay preacher to the seamen in Chatham Dockyard, living with his family on a hulk moored on the River Medway. In 1560, he became the vicar of Upchurch, a small nearby riverside village. The young Francis first learned his seafaring skills on the Medway. The picture above shows Upnor Castle, built for Elizabeth I in 1559–1567 to defend the new dockyard in Chatham.

DRAKE'S ISLAND

Following riots by Catholics in the West Country in 1549, Edmund Drake was forced to leave his home with his family and seek refuge on Saint Nicholas' Island, in Plymouth Harbour. From there, his relative William Hawkins arranged for his safe removal to Kent. The island was afterward known as "Drake's Island" to commemorate the event.

CHILDHOOD HOME

Francis Drake was born in a small farm cottage in Crowndale, near Tavistock in Devon, England, some time between 1539 and 1545, the eldest of 12 children. His father Edmund had been a sailor but had settled on his brother John's farm in 1544. This statue was later erected in Tavistock in honor of Drake's achievements.

A TRADE OF MISERY

John Hawkins, a prominent figure in Elizabeth I's navy, began his well-known career (like Drake himself and many others) by trading slaves, in 1562. Drake's first such voyage was as purser aboard one of Hawkins' ships in 1566. The voyage itself ended in disaster, but Drake went on to become an officer serving with Hawkins on a later slave-trading trip and, in 1568, took command of his first ship.

LANDED GENTRY

Following his knighthood in 1581, Drake boosted his status by claiming to be descended from a Devonshire landed family of the same name. He had their coat of arms displayed aboard his ship, the *Golden Hind*. This is a replica of the *Golden Hind*, which can be seen in London, England.

SIR FRANCIS DRAKE
-A TIMELINE-

~1492~
Columbus's first voyage to the West Indies

~1519~
Magellan sets out on first circumnavigation of the world

~1533~
Princess Elizabeth (later Elizabeth I) is born

~1534~
Cartier's first voyage to Newfoundland

~C. 1535~
Martin Frobisher is born

IRISH REVOLTS

In 1573, on his return from an especially successful raid on Spanish ships in the Caribbean, Drake was obliged to go to Ireland rather than return home. Elizabeth had struck a temporary peace with Spain and his presence in England would have been an embarrassment. He stayed in Ireland for three years, helping Walter Devereux, the 1st Earl of Essex, put down Irish opposition to English colonization. The mission failed, eventually leading to open revolt, during which many English settlers were killed.

JACQUES CARTIER (1491–1557)

Jacques Cartier was a French explorer, commissioned by the king of France to search for possible sites for new settlements in North America and for a Northwest Passage. He made several memorable excursions into the waterways around northeast America and, in 1534, circumnavigated the Gulf of Saint Lawrence. This was thought at the time to be a gateway to the Pacific but turned out to be a huge bay off eastern Canada. He is seen here on a later expedition in 1542, landing on the banks of the mighty Saint Lawrence River. Cartier's explorations led to the later French claims on Canada.

SIR FRANCIS DRAKE
-A TIMELINE-

~1541~

Probable year of Drake's birth in Tavistock, Devon, England

~1545~

Henry VIII's ship, the Mary Rose, sinks

~1547~

Henry VIII dies and is succeeded by Edward VI

~1549~

Cranmer's English Prayer Book published, leads to Catholic riots

Drake family (Protestants) forced to leave Devon for Kent

INHOSPITABLE SEAS

The seas of the northern Atlantic and Arctic Oceans are very inhospitable. Icebergs were a particular problem, and huge areas iced over completely in the winter. This made it difficult for early explorers to chart the northern coasts of America and Russia. Ironically, what none of them knew was that the search for both the Northeast and Northwest passages ultimately led to the same place (later named the Bering Strait), which is the only passage into the northern Pacific Ocean, between Alaska and Siberia.

The Search for the
Northeast & Northwest Passages

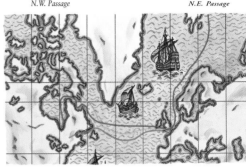

Together, Spain and Portugal controlled the southern seaways, forcing other nations to search for an alternative route to reach the Pacific Ocean and the fabled riches of China and Southeast Asia. Two possibilities emerged: the Northeast Passage, traversing the northern coasts of Russia, and the Northwest Passage, passing around the northern coasts of North America. Drake himself tried unsuccessfully to locate the Northwest Passage, from the Pacific side, in 1578. Having completed his mission to attack Spanish ports on the west coast of South America, he struck north to find

— *Frobisher (1576)* — *Barents (1596)* — *Hudson (1610-11)* — *Cartier (1534-6)*

a way home but was forced back across the Pacific Ocean, and so sailed home around the world, though that was never his original intention. Several navigators in succeeding centuries managed to locate the strait between Alaska and Russia, but none was able to pass through it from the northwest. The Norwegian explorer, Roald Amundsen, is generally accepted to be the first person to sail round northern Canada and through the Bering Strait in 1906, after a three-year expedition.

THE FUR TRADE

Denied the lucrative markets of China and the Far East, merchants soon realized the potential of the fur trade (and later gold) to be found in North America. Large companies were established, such as the Hudson's Bay Company, which made huge profits by buying animal pelts from the Native Americans at very low prices and then exporting them to Europe.

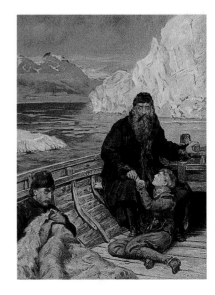

HENRY HUDSON

Henry Hudson (d. 1611) was an English navigator and explorer who was employed by the Dutch East India Company to search for the Northwest Passage. After several attempts, he reached the North American coast and discovered what are now known as the Hudson River, Hudson Strait, and Hudson Bay. In 1611, after a winter spent icebound, his crew mutinied and cast him adrift in a small boat, along with eight others, and he was never seen again.

NEAR MISS

One of the problems facing 16th-century explorers was that the lands for which they were searching were completely unknown, both in terms of location and size. When we trace the routes that they followed, we can see just how close to their objectives they sometimes got, without ever realizing it. On his return journey home around the world, for example, Drake sailed a zigzag course through the East Indies in a vain search for the Southern Continent, taking him tantalizingly close to Australia's northern coast.

SIR FRANCIS DRAKE
-A TIMELINE-

~1553~

Edward VI dies and is succeeded by Mary I

Sir Hugh Willoughby leads expedition to find the Northeast Passage

~1554~

Richard Chancellor reaches Moscow and establishes trade relations with Russia

Mary I marries Philip of Spain

~1558~

Mary I dies and is succeeded by Elizabeth I

~1559~

Elizabeth I is crowned queen of England

Elizabethan Prayer Book published

~1560~

Catholicism outlawed in Scotland

Edmund Drake (Francis's father) takes up the vicarage of Upchurch, Kent, England

TRAVELING IN STYLE

Drake's ship on his circumnavigation was originally called the *Pelican*, but he renamed it *Golden Hind* off South America, before attempting his epic voyage across the southern oceans. This was in honor of his patron Sir Christopher Hatton, whose coat of arms included a hind. Drake enjoyed good living and often carried musicians to entertain him on the long months spent on board ship.

CENTER OF THE UNIVERSE

In Elizabethan times, the other planets in our solar system were thought to revolve around Earth. Armillary spheres (*right*) were used to demonstrate the movements of the heavenly bodies and to show the relative positions of the equator, the tropics, and the Arctic and Antarctic circles. After Magellan's expedition successfully circumnavigated the world, it became possible to calculate Earth's size more accurately and to draw more precise navigational charts.

THE FIRST ENGLISHMAN IN JAPAN

The Elizabethan pilot and adventurer Will Adams set sail in 1598 with a Dutch expedition to Southeast Asia. Only one of the five ships that set out survived, blown off course and eventually landing in Japan in 1600. Adams was taken prisoner but was later released on the condition that he taught the Japanese his seafaring skills. James Clavell's novel *Shogun* is based on Adams' exploits.

QUEST FOR THE SOUTHERN CONTINENT

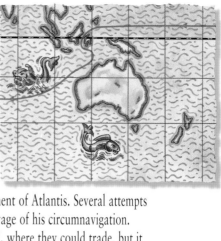

While few Europeans suspected the existence of North and South America in the 1500s (China was believed to lie due west across the Atlantic Ocean), legends abounded of a giant "Southern Continent" somewhere in the south Atlantic Ocean, which many presumed to be the fabled lost continent of Atlantis. Several attempts at discovery were made, including one by Drake on the return voyage of his circumnavigation. Explorers hoped to discover an inhabited and highly civilized land, where they could trade, but it remained elusive. At the same time, the merchant adventurers were also looking to forge trading links with Southeast Asia, in particular the Spice Islands, China, and Japan. The first Englishman to set foot in Japan was Will Adams. Born in Gillingham, in Kent, England, he learned his seafaring skills on the River Medway, like Drake before him. By the end of the 1500s, Spain's "golden age" was coming to a close. Most of the discoveries made after then were by English, Dutch, and French expeditions.

ELUSIVE CONTINENT

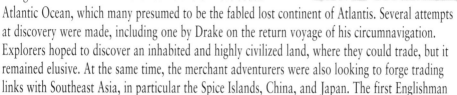

Although a few explorers had made brief contact with the islands to the north of Australia, the existence of an inhabited southern continent eluded the Elizabethans. Abel Tasman landed in Australia in 1642 (below), but it was not until the voyages of Captain Cook, 1768–1780, that the existence of a huge, habitable continent (where we now know Antarctica to be), was finally disproved and the full outline of Australia confirmed.

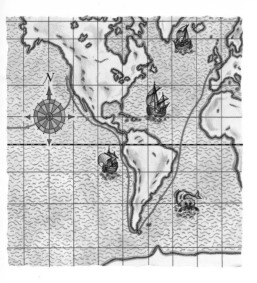

DRAKE'S CIRCUMNAVIGATION OF THE WORLD

Francis Drake was only the second commander (and the first Englishman) successfully to circumnavigate the world. The main reason for Drake's epic journey, however, was not in the interests of scientific discovery but of trade and plunder, motivated by greed. At the time, Spain was the most powerful nation in Europe and jealously guarded the seaways to its lucrative new colonies. Elizabeth I commissioned Drake to sail across the southern Atlantic Ocean, through the Straits of Magellan, and to attack Spanish treasure ships and settlements on South America's unprotected west coast. He then went on to cross the Pacific Ocean and reach the Spice Islands of the East Indies. Drake returned home a rich man, his successful circumnavigation being little more than a boost to his reputation.

"THE DRAGON"

Drake was a powerful personality and commanded respect wherever he went. Native peoples often paid homage to him, and even the Spanish grudgingly referred to him as *El Draque,* "the Dragon," supposedly blessed with magical powers.

REPRISALS

The dangers of native reprisals facing Drake and other explorers —and, indeed, the Spanish settlers—were ever-present. Here, Brazilian cannibals are shown allowing missionaries to baptize their prisoners, but only with a damp cloth so as not to spoil the flavor.

LOST CIVILIZATION

The Maya civilization of Central America flourished many centuries before Drake's circumnavigation. The Maya evolved a sophisticated knowledge of astronomy and mathematics, but there is no evidence that Drake brought back any scientific discoveries from the cities that he visited. Like the Spanish, he merely plundered their riches. The round tower shown here is an observatory in the Mexican city of Chichen Itza.

SPANISH GOLD

The Spaniards ruthlessly exploited the nations of Central and South America, plundering their riches. They melted down gold ornaments and set natives to work in gold and silver mines. The wealth that they shipped back to Spain aroused the interest of Drake and the other Elizabethan privateers. The coins shown here are doubloons (meaning a double or two-escudo piece), the highest value Spanish coin at that time.

NEW ALBION

Drake visited what is now San Francisco to refit his ships before commencing the return journey home. He had an audience with the local Native Americans, who invited him to become their king. He refused but did claim the area for England (calling it New Albion), though no English settlement was ever established there. The Spanish, who made several explorations up the Californian coast, did establish a small missionary settlement there by the bay, which they called San Francisco.

AZTEC SPLENDOR

This picture of Tenochtitlan, in Mexico, shows a pre-conquest view of the magnificent Aztec capital city. Although Drake never reached this far inland—concentrating his efforts on coastal ports—he was just as guilty as the Spaniards in plundering the riches of such ancient sites, principally taking their gold.

SIR FRANCIS DRAKE
-A TIMELINE-

~1562~
John Hawkins' first successful slave-trade voyage to West Indies

~1564~
William Shakespeare born

~1565~
Tobacco first introduced into England—probably by John Hawkins

~1566~
Drake's first voyage to the Caribbean as junior officer on Hawkins' third slave-trade voyage to the Spanish Main

~1568~
Mary Queen of Scots flees to England in exile

The Hawkins/Drake slaving voyage ends in disaster at San Juan de Ulua

~1569~
Drake marries Mary Newman in Saint Budeaux, near Plymouth, England

~1570~
Drake sails for the coast of Panama and begins his reign of terror among Spanish shipping

~1571~
Elizabeth I opens Royal Exchange in London

~1572~
Drake sets out to take the Spanish port of Nombre de Dios, in Panama

~1573~
Peace is agreed between England and Spain—Drake has to lie low with his spoils of war

SIR FRANCIS DRAKE -A TIMELINE-

~1575~

*Drake appears in Ireland
as part of the Earl of
Essex's campaign*

~1576~

*Martin Frobisher attempts
to find Northwest Passage*

*Drake returns from
Ireland and plans his
attack on the west coast
of South America
(this became his
circumnavigation voyage)*

~1577~

*Drake sets out on his
voyage around the world*

*John Hawkins becomes
Treasurer of the Navy
until his death*

SEARCH FOR THE WAY HOME

There is some argument surrounding the exact route home taken by Drake. Some claim that he did not touch land again after leaving Java until arriving back in Plymouth. Others believe that he may have visited southern India before crossing the Indian Ocean. He is seen here apparently paying homage to an Indian ruler.

THE *GOLDEN HIND*

Drake set sail from Plymouth on December 13, 1577 with five ships and a combined crew of 164. The flagship was the *Pelican*, a relatively small vessel of 120 tons carrying just 18 cannon. The smallest ship, the *Benedict*, displaced just 15 tons, a tiny vessel to undertake so difficult a journey. Around halfway into the journey, Drake abandoned two of his ships, probably because of high mortality among the crews. Of the other three, the *Marigold* perished, and the *Elizabeth*, unbeknown to Drake, returned to England without completing the voyage. Only the flagship, renamed the *Golden Hind*, completed the circumnavigation.

KNIGHTHOOD

On Francis Drake's return from his circumnavigation of the world (1577–1580), he was given a hero's welcome. He was knighted by Elizabeth I aboard his ship, the *Golden Hind*, the following year.

BAD FEELING

The serpent and beasts shown here are taken from a collection of engravings made to commemorate Drake's epic voyage. The serpent is a universal symbol of evil and bad luck. Drake's men would have encountered several on the trip, which would have made them very ill-at-ease. Drake kept his intended destination a secret from his men, but when they eventually realized the truth, discontent spread through the crews. They were incited to mutiny by Thomas Doughty, who was put on trial and executed.

THE WAY HOME

Although usually credited as the second person to sail around the world (after Magellan, 1519–1521), Drake actually deserves more credit for his feat than he is sometimes given. Magellan was the first European to cross the Pacific Ocean, but he never completed the circumnavigation of the world himself, though 18 members of his expedition did return to Spain aboard his ship, the *Victoria*. It now seems likely that Magellan's original intention was simply to sail to the East Indies via the Pacific Ocean and that it only became necessary to return home around the world to escape attack from the Portuguese. He was killed in the Philippines after completing around half of the journey, which means that Drake was the first commander to successfully complete a circumnavigation himself.

SECRET VOYAGE

Shortly before embarking on his epic voyage, Drake was summoned to a secret meeting with Queen Elizabeth. She apparently instructed him to raid the unprotected Spanish ports on the west coast of South America. To that end, Drake was extremely successful and brought his investors an incredible 4,700 percent profit. Elizabeth herself profited by £300,000 ($500,000). Drake's first words when he returned to Plymouth on September 26, 1580 were reputedly, "Does the Queen still live?"

EXOTIC NEW FOODS

It was impossible for Drake to take on board all the supplies that he needed for his voyage, so rations were supplemented en route with exotic foods such as the pineapple, which is a native fruit of Central and South America. Other foods from the tropics included coconuts, bananas, and tomatoes. Drake brought back these foods, among many others, to England, where they quickly became eagerly sought as delicacies at the table. Some could be grown in England, but pineapples could only survive in conservatories. Pineapples also became a favorite model for architectural features after this date.

THE NEW COLONIES

The idea of establishing new colonies around the world came slowly to the Elizabethans. The original motivation for exploring new countries arose first out of trade and the need to establish new markets, and second from greed. Even the Spaniards, who actually invaded parts of Central and South America, had little thought of colonization at first—what they craved was gold. England, the Netherlands, and France were quick to follow and readily plundered the

Spanish ships returning home for their share of the booty. It was another 200 years before England made any serious attempts at building an empire. When it did come, it followed the same pattern of establishing colonies around trading posts, with the result that the British Empire was scattered right across the globe along trade routes, rather than radiating out from a logical center.

VIRGINIA

England's first efforts at establishing colonies in North America failed, though they paved the way for later attempts and laid the foundations of what would one day become the British Empire. Walter Raleigh established a small colony in Roanoke Island (now part of North Carolina) in 1584–1585 and christened the territory "Virginia," in honor of Elizabeth, the "virgin queen." Conditions proved too harsh, and the colonists met with hostile reactions from the local Native Americans, resulting in the colony being deserted by 1590.

CONQUISTADORS

At the time of the first European colonization of Central and South America, there were two dominant civilizations there: the Aztecs, centered in what is now Mexico, and the Incas of Peru and surrounding areas. Although technologically advanced, both societies were based on conquest and empire building, rather than colonization, and demanded tribute from those that they defeated. Their society was one of domination—principally by high taxation to pay for monumental works, and their religions demanded sacrificial victims. When the Spanish conquered their lands in the 1500s, many of the ordinary people are said to have welcomed them, initially, as liberators rather than as conquerors (conquistadors).

FAILED COLONY

Following the failure of Raleigh's colony in Roanoke Island, no further attempts at colonization were made by the Elizabethans. The colony of Virginia was eventually re-established farther north and named Jamestown, after James I. This settlement was more successful, based on a thriving tobacco trade with England.

SAVED BY A PRINCESS

One of the early Virginian colonists, Captain John Smith, befriended a Native American princess, Pocahontas. Her father was Powhattan, said to be the king of all the tribes in the area, who remained suspicious of the English. Powhattan decided to slay all the white colonists and return the land to Native American rule, but Pocahontas risked her life to warn Smith and so avoided a massacre.

POCAHONTAS

Although Pocahontas saved the life of John Smith, he was hurt in the struggle and was afterward sent home to England. She later married another prominent colonist, John Rolfe, and traveled to England with him, where she was received at the court of King James I. Pocahontas persuaded Rolfe to let her return to America, but tragically, at the age of 22 she died on the eve of her departure (May 2, 1617) from either smallpox or a common cold and is buried in Gravesend, in Kent, England.

NATIVE AMERICANS' REVENGE

The Spanish conquerors of Central and South America overran the local Native Americans within just two years. Unfortunately, before any real attempts at colonization had been contemplated, the Spanish thirst for gold (which was in plentiful supply and was regarded by the Native Americans as only of decorative value) reached its peak. The conquerors openly pillaged the land, Mexico and Peru in particular, in their search for riches. Although initially welcomed by the Native Americans as saviors from a harsh military regime, the Spaniards soon took advantage and exploited the Native Americans, killing and torturing thousands. Then they enslaved thousands more in the silver mines that they discovered. Native Americans are here seen extracting their revenge by pouring molten gold down the throat of a captured conquistador.

THE SPANISH INVASION

One of the reasons for the speed with which Spain overran the Aztec and Inca empires is that many conquered Native American tribes, hostile to their old enemies, actively aided the Spanish soldiers. Another reason was the Spanish use of guns, which were unheard of in South America. Cortés conquered the Aztec civilization in 1519–1520, completely destroying their capital of Tenochtitlan in the process, and building his own capital, Mexico City, on its ruins.

NEW TRADE ROUTES

The need to discover new trade routes during Elizabeth I's reign grew directly out of England's ongoing war with Spain. Spain was then the richest and most powerful country in Europe and had already extended its empire to much of the West Indies and Central America, jealously guarding the southern and western seaways. International trade was as important to the Elizabethan economy and society as it is to us today, and so it became essential to open up new trade routes. Even though traveling by sea was hazardous, it was still preferable to overland transportation, which was hindered by poor roads and hostile countries. Drake and the other Elizabethan seafarers began by simply stealing Spanish treasure and other blatant acts of piracy, but soon the need to open up new and longer term trade routes became the priority.

THE SLAVE TRADE

The Spanish occupation of the Caribbean and South America had been ruthless, and many native people were killed. Many of the survivors proved unsuitable or unwilling to be employed as laborers, so there was a ready market for slaves exported from West Africa. The Spaniards strictly controlled the import of slaves into the colonies, but English mariners, including Drake and Hawkins, engaged in illicit slave trading to the Spanish Main and, afterward, to the new colonies of North America.

A SWEET TOOTH

Prior to the 1500s, sugar had been available in England in the form of sugar beet (a root vegetable), but extraction was laborious. Sugar cane yielded a much more productive crop, but it would not grow in the English climate. Many sugar plantations were established in the West Indies, usually employing slave labor.

SOUTH CHINA SEAS

Opening up new trade routes was not without its problems. From the mid-1500s on, trade between the Far East and Europe increased dramatically, so much so that heavily laden merchant ships soon became prime targets for pirate attacks. The South China Seas between China, Japan, and the East Indies were particularly treacherous. Sometimes fleets of pirate vessels descended upon merchant ships. Favorite vessels of Chinese pirates were captured, including trading junks, as shown here, converted to carry guns. Eventually, influential merchant companies (such as the East India Company), who financed the voyages, persuaded the British government to protect merchant shipping.

RUSSIA

In 1553, Sir Hugh Willoughby and Richard Chancellor set out to try to discover the Northeast Passage. They became separated. Willoughby perished in the ice, but Chancellor went on to reach the Russian coast and then traveled overland to Moscow *(right)* the following year. He set up trade relations (principally in furs) between Russia and England, but died just off Scotland on a return trip in 1555.

UNUSUAL FOODS

Many of the foods, such as the tomato, brought back by the Elizabethan seafarers were regarded as no more than interesting curiosities. Others, like the potato, quickly became favorites at the table to supplement the often limited diet of the time. They were usually expensive, however, and so were regarded more as a delicacy until botanists succeeded in growing the plants in the English climate. The introduction of culinary spices brought back from abroad was welcomed. Peppers and chilies *(left)*, from South America, were used to disguise the often rancid taste of Elizabethan food, while from the East Indies came such flavorings as cloves. During Drake's circumnavigation, he had to take on board many unusual and exotic foods to sustain his crews. Among these was the coconut palm, which natives used as a major source of food, making oil from the kernels. Drake brought a coconut back to England, which he presented to Elizabeth as a memento of his voyage. The tobacco plant *(above right)* came from North America, where the Native Americans smoked it in clay pipes. Originally, it was used as a medicine to purge the body of phlegm.

TOWARD AN EMPIRE

SIR THOMAS GRESHAM
(c. 1519–1579)

The cost of voyages abroad was very high and could not have been undertaken without financial backing from rich merchants. One of the foremost was Sir Thomas Gresham, who built the Royal Exchange in London, England.

Elizabethan expeditions looking for new trade routes reached destinations as far apart as Russia, North America, and Canada in the north, and South America, Africa, and Asia in the south. Their achievement was all the more incredible because of the length of time taken to complete the journeys in small vessels, often crossing uncharted seas. The importance of opening up new trade routes to Asia and the East Indies was paramount in the eyes of the Elizabethan merchant adventurers. Spices were the most prized and valuable commodity, fetching enormous prices on the European markets.

The view shown here is of the tropical coast of Ceylon, now Sri Lanka, off the southeast coast of India.

THE BEGINNINGS OF AN EMPIRE

India and Ceylon had been known to European explorers since
at least the time of Marco Polo (c. 1254–1324) and would have
been familiar to the Elizabethan seafarers on their frequent visits
to the Spice Islands. As elsewhere, the Elizabethans' prime
concern was setting up new trade routes, but they frequently
encountered strange new cultures, from Native American
witch doctors in North America (shown here) to the highly
sophisticated and ancient cultures of Asia. In 1601, the East
India Company received its royal charter,
marking the beginning of
Great Britain's first
claims to an empire.

SHIPS & SAILING

The crews of the early voyages of exploration faced many dangers. Not only did they have to put up with cramped conditions and only a small supply of food and water (which was often bad), but they were sailing into the unknown with little idea where they were and how fast they were traveling. Perhaps it is not surprising, therefore, that Columbus and others often had to face mutiny. Today, ships have little trouble locating their exact position. Accurate maps, clocks, and global positioning satellites (GPS) mean that sailors can tell where they are to within a few feet. Sailors in the 1400s and 1500s were not so fortunate.

MAGNETIC COMPASS

It was vitally important that the sailors crossing the Atlantic Ocean knew exactly in what direction they were sailing. On a clear day or night, either the Sun or the North Star were used. They could also use a magnetic compass. The magnetic field around Earth meant that a magnetized needle floating in water would always point northward.

DEAD RECKONING

If a navigator knew where his ship sailed from, what its speed was, the direction the ship was traveling in, and how long they had been traveling, then it was possible to calculate how far they had traveled by "dead-reckoning" and so find their position. However, winds and tides meant that this was only an approximate way of figuring out the ship's position.

THE ASTROLABE

Every navigator in Elizabethan times made use of the astrolabe (similar to this Arabic example). It could be used to find out how far north or south of the equator (latitude) the ship was. It worked by measuring the height of the North Star or noon Sun from the ship. Once the height was known, then the navigator could calculate how far north or south he was.

THE CROSS-STAFF

The simplest way to measure the latitude of a ship was to use an instrument called a cross-staff. It had a crossbar for sighting and a rod with measurements cut into the side. The crossbar would be lined up between the Sun or North Star and the horizon. The measurements of the long piece of wood would then tell the navigator the angle of the Sun or star from the horizon. From this, he could figure out his latitude. There is considerable danger in staring at the Sun for too long. In 1595, Captain John Davis invented the back-staff, which used mirrors and shadows so that navigators did not risk being injured.

TELLING THE TIME

For the navigator to calculate a ship's position, it was vital that he knew what time of day it was. Sailors would be given the job of watching a large sand-filled hourglass (similar to this 17th-century example, shown here). It normally emptied after 30 minutes and then a bell would be rung so that everybody on board knew what the time was.

THE QUADRANT

Alongside the astrolabe, Elizabethan explorers often took quadrants with them. When Ferdinand Magellan started on his famous voyage around the world in 1519, he took seven astrolabes and 21 quadrants. Quadrants did basically the same job as astrolabes. They worked by lining up one arm with the horizon and then moving a movable arm so that it was pointing at either the Sun or North Star. The angle between these two arms could then be used to calculate the ship's latitude. It could only really work when the sea was calm and still.

NAVIGATION

In these days of radar, GPS, and satellites, it is easy to underestimate the great navigational skills of the Elizabethan seafarers. For the most part, they were sailing uncharted seas and had to estimate their position as best as they could, using only the positions of heavenly bodies to guide them. Until the development of more refined instruments, such as the chronometer in the mid-1700s, navigation was a very inexact science and relied heavily on the observational skills of the individual. Needless to say, there were many accidents, especially if the ships were blown off-course by bad weather into unknown waters.

GUIDED BY THE STARS

During the 1500s, the cross-staff became commonly used to calculate a ship's latitude (north-south position) at night. It comprised two pieces of wood, similar in appearance to a crossbow, with graduated scales marked along the length. By observing the angle between the horizon and the North (or Pole) Star and taking a reading off the scale, coupled with a compass reading, the ship's approximate position could be calculated. Shown here is a buckstaff, invented around 1594, for measuring the height of the Sun for the same purpose.

THE "MARINER'S MIRROUR"

Following Magellan's, and later Drake's, circumnavigation of the world, it became possible to assess Earth's size more accurately. This led in turn to the production of more accurate charts. The first sea atlas to be published in England, in 1588, was the *Mariner's Mirrour*. It was a collection of maps and charts derived from Dutch originals showing the known coastlines of the world. At the time, the Dutch were an English ally against Spain and at the forefront of navigational techniques.

LODESTONE

One of the main problems facing Elizabethan navigators was accurately calculating a ship's longitude (east–west position). Here, the astronomer–mathematician Flavius tries to do so by floating a piece of lodestone (a form of iron oxide) in a bowl of water, while making calculations.

STEERING BY THE SUN

This scene shows an Elizabethan navigator trying to calculate the ship's latitude by use of a compass and an early form of quadrant to measure the angle of the Sun's rays. However, precise timekeeping was necessary to ensure the accuracy of the calculations, so at best a ship's position could only be approximated. The first fully successful sea clock (chronometer) was not developed until 1759.

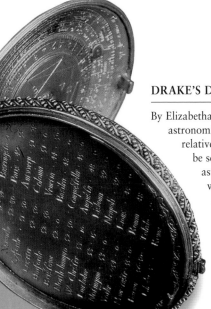

DRAKE'S DIAL

By Elizabethan times, compasses and other astronomical instruments had become relatively sophisticated, as can be seen in this beautifully crafted astronomical compendium. It was made of brass in 1569 by Humphrey Cole, one of the finest scientific instrument makers of the time, and was once believed to have belonged to Drake himself. The compendium comprised a compass, along with lunar and solar dials, which, as well as being an astronomical aid, enabled the user to calculate the time. Engraved on the casing were the latitudes of many important ports around the world.

SIR FRANCIS DRAKE
-A TIMELINE-

~1583~
Sir Humphrey Gilbert claims Newfoundland for England

~1584~
Walter Raleigh establishes the first colony in Virginia

~1585~
Drake raids Santiago

Drake sets sail for West Indies, his first command as admiral

~1587~
Mary Queen of Scots executed

~1587~
The Spanish decide to launch offensive against England

GETTING YOUR BEARINGS

The ancient Chinese discovered that lodestone is naturally magnetic and if suspended on a string will always point to the north. Early navigators made good use of this natural material, but it was somewhat crude. Sometime in the 1100s, European navigators discovered that a needle could be similarly magnetised by stroking it with a lodestone. This discovery eventually led to the development of more sophisticated and accurate compasses, with the needle balanced on a central pivot. The example shown here is encased in an ivory bowl and dates from around 1580.

LIFE ON BOARD

Life on board a ship in Elizabethan times was extremely harsh, and the pay (which was frequently in arrears) was very bad. But, faced with extremely bad poverty on land at a time when many country people were being forcibly ejected from their land because of changing farming practices, many had little option. A fair proportion of a ship's crew would also have been criminals escaping justice, which often led to problems with discipline. The mortality rate among an average crew was very high, and it would be considered normal for a ship to return to port with only one quarter of the men left alive. To ensure that they had enough men left to make the return journey, most captains oversubscribed when signing on a new crew, but this in itself led to problems of overcrowding and food rationing. Conditions on board were cramped, each man usually sleeping in a hammock slung below decks at his place of work. Bathroom facilities were virtually nonexistent.

JACK-OF-ALL-TRADES

A crew on an Elizabethan ship had to be completely self-sufficient, for they were often away at sea for several years and might go many months between landings. As well as being able to handle the ship, sailors had to master other essential skills, such as carpentry, sailmaking, ropemaking, and cooking.

DRUNKENNESS

Two of the most common problems facing any captain commanding an Elizabethan ship on a long voyage were boredom and the unruly behavior of his crew. With fresh water in short supply, the only drink available was beer (a gallon per crew member per day) or other stronger alcohols, which frequently led to drunkenness, not only on board but also in port. Discipline was necessarily very harsh in order to avoid potentially fatal accidents at sea.

DISEASES

The most common form of disease encountered aboard ship was scurvy, a deficiency of vitamin C, caused by lack of fresh fruit and vegetables. The symptoms include bleeding into the skin and the loosening of teeth. Resistance to infection is also lowered, often resulting in death if untreated. All ships carried their share of rats, which might spread infectious diseases such as plague. Other common diseases were malaria, typhoid, and dysentery.

THE CHATHAM CHEST

After the Armada of 1588, so many seamen were wounded and maimed that Sir John Hawkins established the "Chatham Chest"—the first seamen's charity. All sailors in the Navy had to pay six pence per month from their wages into it for welfare purposes. This is the chest of 1625.

THE ART OF THE GUNNER

Most Elizabethan ships carried a number of cannon (a mortar is shown left), usually made from cast iron or bronze. They were mounted on carriages and secured in place by heavy ropes to control the recoil when being fired and to prevent them from coming adrift in heavy seas. They were mostly used to disable a ship before boarding.

HEALTH AND SAFETY

The health and safety of the crew aboard a typical Elizabethan ship was, to say the least, extremely hazardous. There were many accidents while simply carrying out the day-to-day tasks of sailing. Injuries sustained during encounters with enemy vessels, usually at close quarters, were horrific. Most ships carried a surgeon, but the treatment he was able to administer was both limited and very crude. By far the most common form of treatment was the amputation of badly damaged or infected limbs. There was no anesthetic (other than to make the patient drunk) and the survival rate was appallingly low. Many of those who survived surgery died from gangrene afterward.

DAILY SUSTENANCE

All of the ship's food was prepared in the galley and then distributed among the crew. Food was rarely fresh and might consist of a crackerlike biscuit, salted beef or fish, supplemented by cheese and gruel, a type of porridge mix. Drinking water was usually scarce, but most ships carried a plentiful supply of beer. The pieces of tableware shown here were retrieved from Henry VIII's ship the *Mary Rose* and are typical of items in use throughout the Tudor period.

THE SPANISH ARMADA

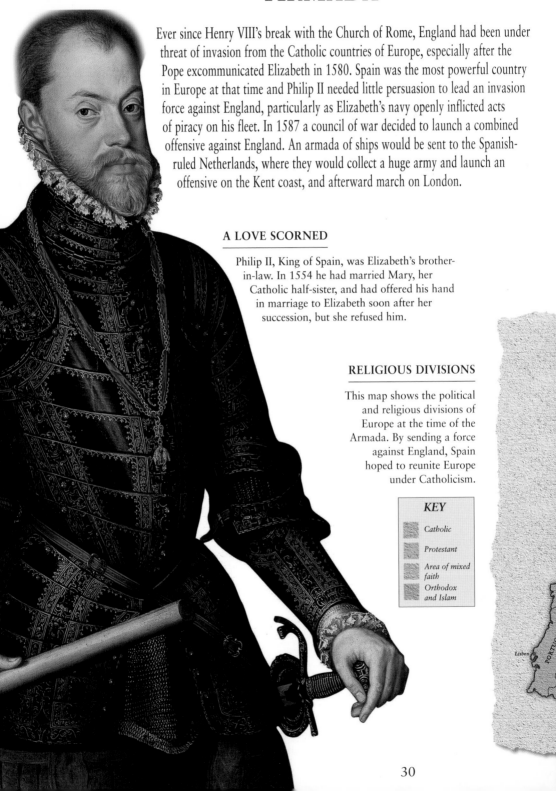

Ever since Henry VIII's break with the Church of Rome, England had been under threat of invasion from the Catholic countries of Europe, especially after the Pope excommunicated Elizabeth in 1580. Spain was the most powerful country in Europe at that time and Philip II needed little persuasion to lead an invasion force against England, particularly as Elizabeth's navy openly inflicted acts of piracy on his fleet. In 1587 a council of war decided to launch a combined offensive against England. An armada of ships would be sent to the Spanish-ruled Netherlands, where they would collect a huge army and launch an offensive on the Kent coast, and afterward march on London.

A LOVE SCORNED

Philip II, King of Spain, was Elizabeth's brother-in-law. In 1554 he had married Mary, her Catholic half-sister, and had offered his hand in marriage to Elizabeth soon after her succession, but she refused him.

RELIGIOUS DIVISIONS

This map shows the political and religious divisions of Europe at the time of the Armada. By sending a force against England, Spain hoped to reunite Europe under Catholicism.

KEY

Catholic

Protestant

Area of mixed faith

Orthodox and Islam

Lisbon PORTUGAL

EARLY WARNING SYSTEM

A system of beacons around the coast warned of the Armada's approach. Each beacon, within sight of its neighbors, could convey a warning the length of the country in minutes.

DRAKE ACQUIRES HIS SEA LEGS

Sir Francis Drake was born at Tavistock, Devon, in c.1541, though he learned his seafaring skills on the River Medway, in Kent, after his father, a naval chaplain, transferred to Chatham Dockyard around 1550.

THE ROUTE OF THE ARMADA

The map above shows the route taken by the Armada. It set out from Lisbon on May 20, 1588 only to be scattered by bad weather. On July 12, after revictualing and repairs, it set out again from La Coruna, in northern Spain, arriving in the Channel, off the Scilly Isles, on July 19.

PITCHED BATTLE

The commander of the English fleet sent
to stop the Armada was Lord Howard of
Effingham. A week-long pitched battle took
place in the Channel, but the English could
not halt the progress of the Spanish. The
battle turned in favor of the English,
however, when Drake launched
eight fire ships into the Armada
off Gravelines (north of Calais,
France), which threw the Spanish
into disarray. The following day
the Armada was routed and fled
into the North Sea.

Spanish Defeat

Although the English had given a good account of themselves, the Armada succeeded in reaching its first objective, Calais, where they were to be joined by the Duke of Parma's army to invade England, but Dutch rebels prevented Parma's ships from putting to sea. Of the 138 ships that set out from Spain only 67 returned, most falling victim to the treacherous seas around Scotland and Ireland. The crews were ravaged by hunger and disease. Philip was devastated by the news that his grand plan had failed and, although in a few years his navy was stronger than ever, Spain never fully recovered from the humiliating defeat.

ARMADA MEDAL

This gold medal, commemorating England's victory over the Armada, was awarded to each one of the commanders of the English fleet.

THE FLIGHT OF THE ARMADA

This map shows the route taken by the Armada in retreat. Prevailing winds aided their escape around the coasts of Scotland and Ireland. Howard pursued them for three days before returning home to victory celebrations.

DRAKE—LATER LIFE

DRAKE'S LAST VOYAGE

Drake's last, ill-fated voyage took place in 1595–1596. He and John Hawkins were commanded to attack Puerto Rico, to cut off Spain's supply of treasure ships. There was friction between the two admirals from the start, which came to a head when Drake decided to make an excursion to the Canary Islands *(above)* for supplies. The attack failed, but worse was to come. A messenger ship was sent from the Canaries to warn the governor of Puerto Rico of the intended attack. The island's defenses had been sadly lacking and would probably have succumbed to Drake and Hawkins. But with two weeks' warning, the Spaniards were able to make the necessary preparations, and in the event the English attack failed dismally. Hawkins died before the attack was launched, and Drake died around one month later, of dysentery, on January 25, 1596, off Porto Bello.

Although Drake has often been accused of being a ne'er-do-well who was little better than a legalized pirate, acting as Elizabeth's agent in her war with Spain, such criticism is perhaps a little harsh. He was, by all accounts, an honorable man who took good care of his crews, even if he sometimes used rough methods. He certainly liked the finer things in life and, following his knighthood in 1581, regarded himself as a member of the new aristocracy. This earned him many enemies among those with inherited titles. After his circumnavigation, he became Mayor of Plymouth and campaigned for many improvements to the town, including a better water supply. A short man of stocky build, he is said to have become relatively heavy in later life and settled into semi-retirement at Buckland Abbey, near his birthplace. This had been seized by the crown at the dissolution and converted into a fine house by Sir Richard Grenville.

DRAKE'S DRUM

*"Take my drum to England, hang et by the shore,
Strike et when your powder's runnin' low;
If the Dons sight Devon, I'll quit the port o' Heaven,
An' drum them up the Channel as
we drummed them long ago."*

These lines are an extract from a poem by Sir Henry Newbolt. The drum was used aboard the *Golden Hind* to muster the crew for battle. On his deathbed, Drake, according to legend, promised to return and fight for England if ever the drum were beaten at the approach of an enemy.

EXCELLENT STRATEGIST

Throughout his illustrious career, Drake had struck fear into the hearts of the Spaniards. In 1587, he executed a flawless attack on Cadiz harbor, where he was said to have "singed the King of Spain's beard" by destroying 37 (the Spanish claimed it was 24) galleons gathering to form an armada to be sent against England. The following year, of course, he was instrumental in defeating the "Great Armada" itself and in between times he was a constant threat to Spanish shipping in the Caribbean. An excellent navigator, he revolutionized naval strategy by taking the fight to the enemy. When Philip II of Spain heard news of Drake's death, he is said to have rejoiced openly.

FALL FROM FAVOR

In 1583, Drake's first wife died, and soon after he married Elizabeth Sydenham, who outlived him, but he had no children with either wife. He engaged in a few expeditions following his circumnavigation, but he gradually slipped into semi-retirement following the defeat of the Armada in 1588 and spent more and more time either in London, at court, or in his new official duties in Plymouth. During that time, he fell somewhat from favor, and Martin Frobisher superseded him as Elizabeth I's shining star.

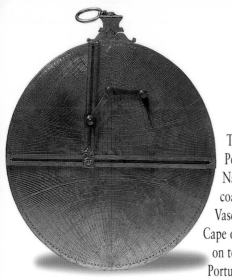

THE ELIZABETHAN EXPLORERS

The "age of discovery" by European explorers really began in Portugal, in 1415, with Prince Henry, known as Henry the Navigator. He sent ships out to explore the north and west coasts of Africa, and they brought back riches such as ivory. Vasco da Gama (c. 1460–1524), also Portuguese, rounded the Cape of Good Hope, off the southernmost tip of Africa, and went on to open the first European maritime route to India. Later Portuguese explorers went on to discover routes to Japan, Southeast Asia, and South America, which soon made Portugal one of the wealthiest nations in Europe. Spain, and later England, followed these first voyages in their thirst for gold and other riches, most of which—except in the Far East—were plundered from the native inhabitants of the countries that they visited. Apart from advances made in compiling more accurate navigational charts, very little scientific data was gathered on these early voyages, which were primarily motivated by money and trade.

ARAB INFLUENCE

Arab explorers from north Africa greatly extended their empire between the 500s and 1200s, as far as northern Spain. They sailed the Mediterranean and the Indian Ocean in small boats called dhows. They developed sophisticated astronomical equipment, such as this astrolabe, that greatly influenced European mariners.

JOHN CABOT (C. 1450–1499)

The quest for new trade routes in Tudor England really began with Henry VII. He considered sponsoring Christopher Columbus on his voyage of discovery to the New World but chose instead to finance an expedition by the Italian John Cabot, who tried to find a new route to China and the Spice Islands via the fabled Northwest Passage. Cabot believed he had reached China when he struck land, but it was in fact the coast of Newfoundland. He is seen here departing from Bristol, England in 1497.

CHURCH MISSIONARIES

Although the prime objective of the early explorers had been money, with no real interest in colonization, the Church had different views. Within a few years of the first expeditions, Christian missionaries were established to convert the pagan natives. Many were not always successful in their cause and fell victim to the Native Americans, like the Franciscan missionaries shown here.

THE SHIPWRIGHT'S SKILL

One of the reasons given for England's superiority at sea over Spain is the design of her warships. Sir John Hawkins was responsible for introducing revolutionary new designs by Matthew Baker and Peter Pett, which completely transformed the English navy. The new ships were smaller and sleeker than the cumbersome Spanish galleons. They were low at the bows but high at the stern, which made them much more maneuvrable.

CELESTIAL GLOBE

This Flemish celestial globe of c. 1537 shows the somewhat limited understanding of the constellations in the skies of the Southern Hemisphere in Tudor times. Information gathered from the around-the-world voyages of Magellan, Drake, and Cavendish was added later, but a lack of knowledge made any journey in the southern oceans especially hazardous.

SIR FRANCIS DRAKE
-A TIMELINE-

~1587~
The Spanish decide to launch offensive against England

Drake sacks the port of Cadiz "singeing the King of Spain's beard"

~1588~
Spanish Armada sent against England and defeated in the Channel after week-long running battle

~1591~
Sir Richard Grenville of the Revenge *dies after being outnumbered by a Spanish fleet in the Azores*

NO SMOKE WITHOUT FIRE

While Raleigh is popularly credited with introducing potatoes and tobacco to England from the New World, that honor is now usually given to his contemporary, Sir John Hawkins. Raleigh did make smoking fashionable at court, however, where he was one of Elizabeth I's favorites. Tobacco was usually smoked in long clay pipes, similar to the pipes used by Native Americans. Raleigh is seen here being doused with water by one of his servants, who feared he was on fire!

SIR WALTER RALEIGH
(C. 1552–1618)

Sir Walter Raleigh was a soldier, courtier, and explorer. He was a leading exponent of establishing English colonies in the New World, including Virginia, but they all failed. When James I acceded to the throne, Raleigh was accused of treason and imprisoned.

SIR FRANCIS DRAKE
- A TIMELINE -

~1593~

Battle of Ballishannon in Ireland

~1594~

Martin Frobisher dies

~1595~

Drake sets off to attack Puerto Rico (his last voyage) with John Hawkins

Sir John Hawkins dies

~1596~

Drake dies of dysentery in Porto Bello in the Caribbean

SIR JOHN HAWKINS
(1532–1595)

Sir John Hawkins, a distant relative of Drake, was responsible for modernizing Elizabeth I's navy and played a major role in defeating the Spanish Armada. After the Armada, many of the crews were unpaid, and together with Drake, Hawkins set up a fund for distressed seamen called the Chatham Chest. He is said to have introduced the potato and tobacco into England. He died in 1595 during his and Drake's last, ill-fated Caribbean voyage.

THE SEARCH FOR EL DORADO

In 1616, while still in prison, Raleigh persuaded James I to let him lead an expedition (his second) to the Orinoco River in Guyana, to search for the fabled El Dorado (City of Gold). The voyage failed, and Raleigh returned home in disgrace. He was executed in 1618 under the original terms of his sentence.

A MYSTERIOUS WORLD

The world in the 1400s was much more fragmented than we would recognize today. Areas of advanced civilization existed in many places, including North Africa, the Mediterranean, China, and India, but each only had a limited knowledge of the existence of the others. Few Europeans at that time had any awareness of the world beyond Europe itself. Legends and travelers' tales abounded, so that even those who did venture farther afield were seldom believed. The Atlantic Ocean was largely unexplored, and the existence of America and the Pacific Ocean beyond had not been proved. Much of the world remained a mystery, uncharted and unmapped. For the brave adventurers setting out on their voyages of discovery, with only limited navigational skills, it was a journey into the unknown, akin to our own space explorations to the Moon and beyond.

SIR RICHARD GRENVILLE (C. 1541–1591)

Sir Richard Grenville was another man who advocated the colonization of the New World rather than simply making piratical raids on Spanish treasure ships. He is best remembered for his gallant fight off Flores, in the Azores, in 1591. He was commander of the *Revenge*, Drake's former flagship against the Armada, and when he found himself surrounded by Spanish vessels, he insisted on carrying on the fight alone. A harsh and arrogant man, he was fatally wounded and ordered the ship to be scuttled rather than to give it up to the Spanish, but his crew insisted on surrendering instead. Grenville died on board the Spanish flagship shortly afterward.

SIR HUMPHREY GILBERT (C. 1539–1583)

Sir Humphrey Gilbert was another leading exponent of establishing English colonies in the New World. In 1578, he received Letters Patent from Elizabeth I authorizing him to colonize new lands. Finally, in 1583, he gathered sufficient support and set off for Newfoundland. In Saint John's, already a flourishing port, he formally claimed the territory for England. He died on the way home, leaving his half-brother, Walter Raleigh, to finish his task.

EPIC VOYAGERS

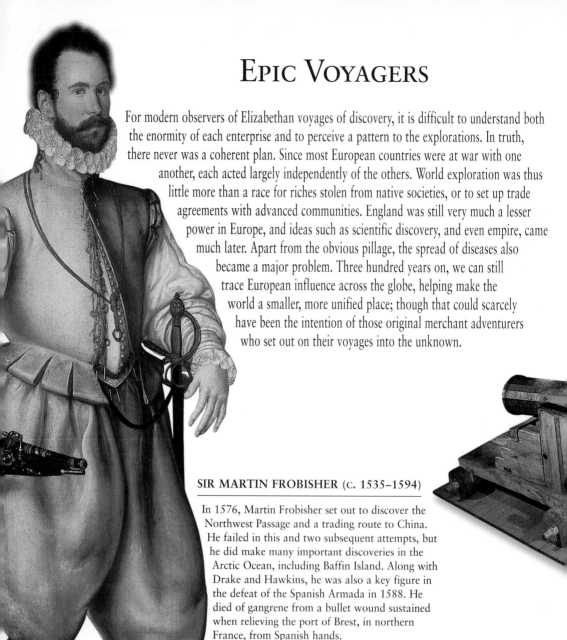

For modern observers of Elizabethan voyages of discovery, it is difficult to understand both the enormity of each enterprise and to perceive a pattern to the explorations. In truth, there never was a coherent plan. Since most European countries were at war with one another, each acted largely independently of the others. World exploration was thus little more than a race for riches stolen from native societies, or to set up trade agreements with advanced communities. England was still very much a lesser power in Europe, and ideas such as scientific discovery, and even empire, came much later. Apart from the obvious pillage, the spread of diseases also became a major problem. Three hundred years on, we can still trace European influence across the globe, helping make the world a smaller, more unified place; though that could scarcely have been the intention of those original merchant adventurers who set out on their voyages into the unknown.

SIR MARTIN FROBISHER (C. 1535–1594)

In 1576, Martin Frobisher set out to discover the Northwest Passage and a trading route to China. He failed in this and two subsequent attempts, but he did make many important discoveries in the Arctic Ocean, including Baffin Island. Along with Drake and Hawkins, he was also a key figure in the defeat of the Spanish Armada in 1588. He died of gangrene from a bullet wound sustained when relieving the port of Brest, in northern France, from Spanish hands.

STRANGE SIGHTS

Explorers in the 1500s encountered strange sights on their intrepid voyages, including many alien cultures and plants and animals never before seen by Europeans. The women shown here (believed to have lived in Java) are killing themselves following the death of their king, an act witnessed by Cavendish on his circumnavigation (1586–1588).

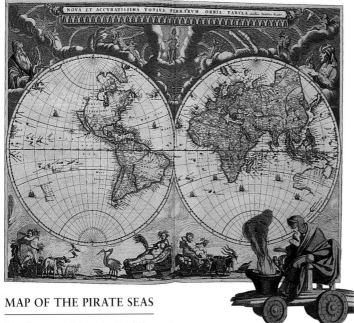

MAP OF THE PIRATE SEAS

The first expeditions by English mariners
were little more than acts of legalized piracy.
Elizabeth I instructed her sea captains to intercept as many Spanish
treasure ships as possible and steal their gold.
Afterward, when the expeditions became
more legitimate, the seas remained infested
by pirates, opportunist cutthroats who
attacked any ship and plundered its cargo.

ARMAMENTS

Most ships in the 1500s carried a small number
of guns, similar to this bronze demi-
cannon that was retrieved from the
wreck of the *Mary Rose*, which sank
in 1545. It was one of the first English
warships to be equipped with gunports
cut into her sides. Cannon of this type
were usually cast from iron or bronze and
remained the principal form of armament
on fighting ships for the next 300 years.

THOMAS CAVENDISH (1560–1592)

Shortly after Drake's return from his circumnavigation of the
world, Thomas Cavendish was commissioned to copy his epic
voyage. He completed the journey in less time than Drake
(1586–1588) but largely followed the same route. His was
probably the first intentional voyage of circumnavigation.
Both Magellan's and Drake's voyages appear to have had
other motives, at least initially, and both were forced to
complete their circumnavigation as the safest route home.
In 1591, Cavendish set out again for the East Indies, but the
voyage ended in disaster. Through the Straits of Magellan the
men killed penguins for sustenance, which putrefied, overrunning
the ship with worms. Soon afterward, an especially bad bout of
scurvy broke out, killing around three-quarters of the crew.

SIR FRANCIS DRAKE
-A TIMELINE-

~1598~
Philip II, King of Spain, dies

~1600~
*Will Adams becomes first
Englishman to land in Japan*

~1603~
*Elizabeth I (last Tudor
monarch) dies and is succeeded
by James I*

Raleigh arrested for treason

~1609~
*Hudson's first expedition
to North America*

~1616~
*Raleigh sets out to discover
El Dorado but fails and
returns to England in disgrace*

~1618~
*Sir Walter Raleigh executed
for treason*

DID YOU KNOW?

How the Spice Islands got their name?

One of the main attractions for the Elizabethan explorers searching for new trade routes were spices from the East. The groups of islands that make up the East Indies (which include the Moluccas, Philippines, and Melanesia groups of islands) were particularly rich in such commodities and came to be known collectively as the Spice Islands.

That of all the continents, Antarctica is the coldest, driest, highest, and windiest?

It covers an area half as large again as the U.S.A. (about 5.5 million sq. mi./14 million sq. km.) and represents one-tenth of Earth's land mass. Approximately 98 percent of Antarctica is covered by ice up to 1.5 mi. (2.4km) thick in places. The Elizabethan explorers had searched in vain for a habitable land mass in the southern oceans, which was not finally discovered until 1820 when Edward Bransfield landed on part of the Antarctic Peninsula.

Where the term "square meal" comes from?

It is not known when this term first came into use but since at least Tudor times meals on board ship were dished up on square platters, that seamen balanced on their laps. They had frames around the edge to prevent the food from falling off and were so shaped to enable them to be easily stored when not in use. Each sailor thus received his full ration, or square meal, for the day.

How America got its name?

America was named after the 16th-century navigator and mapmaker Amerigo Vespucci. Of Italian birth, in 1508 he was created Chief Royal Pilot of Spain. All Spanish captains had to provide him with full details each time they undertook a new voyage so that he could constantly amend and update his collection of sea charts. He made several voyages to the New World himself (notably in 1499–1500) and was once credited with discovering America. Although this was not true, he was the first to consider it to be an independent continent and not part of Asia. It was afterward known as "Amerigo's Land" in his honor.

That legends associated with Drake's Drum (see page 34) are still being created?

During World War II, stories circulated of warships supposedly carrying Drake's Drum that were miraculously saved from disaster after the ghostly sounds of drumming were heard. In truth, the drum has never been carried on board any ship since its return to England in the 1500s. During the World War II it was locked away for safe-keeping. Replicas may have been carried on board ships, but not the original, which shows just how easily stories can generate, especially if spread by word of mouth.

That we still use the stars to navigate by?

It is easy to assume that because navigational techniques used in the past were relatively simple they were also inaccurate. This is not necessarily true, although results need to be accurately recorded and verified to be usable. In 1967 astronomers discovered pulsars—rapidly rotating condensed stars (formed from dead stars) that emit radio waves, or pulses, as detectable beams. Pulsars pulsate at fixed rates, making it possible for future space programs to utilize them for navigational purposes in outer space.

42

What ships the Europeans used as trading vessels?
In the first part of the 1500s the carrack became the most popular European ship for trade, exploration, and warfare. Carracks became important symbols of national pride. In England, Henry VIII had built the *Great Harry*, which was the largest carrack built up until that time. The French responded by building *La Grande Françoise*, which was even larger. Sadly, it was so large that it could not get out of the mouth of the harbor where it was built. By the end of the 1500s the carrack was being replaced by the galleon.

Who made up a ship's crew?
Most ships not only had ordinary sailors among the crew, but also carpenters, priests, cooks, doctors, gunners, blacksmiths, pilots, and boys as young as ten on board. Crew members normally came from many different countries and the captain sometimes had difficulty making them understand his instructions.

What the biggest problem faced by sailors was?
The main problem faced by sailors on long voyages was scurvy. This often fatal disease is caused by a lack of vitamin C which comes from fresh fruit and vegetables. Fresh food did not last long on the ships of the explorers. Sailors would become extremely tired and would start to bleed from the scalp and the gums. However, it was not until 1915 that vitamins were identified. Citrus fruit juice (ascorbic acid) was adopted against scurvy by the Admiralty in 1795, but before that fresh air, dry clothing, warmth, and exercise were also thought to help prevent it. Consequently there was much confusion about the exact cause of scurvy.

How time gives longitude?
Each day (24 hours) the Earth turns through 360°, from west to east; that is, it turns through 15° of longitude every hour and 1° every 4 minutes. A place that has a 4-minute difference in time at noon from a starting point (or prime meridian) to east or west—noon in each spot being when the Sun is exactly overhead—is 1° of longitude away. So, accurate east/west time variations between places can be converted into relative distances and positions of longitude.

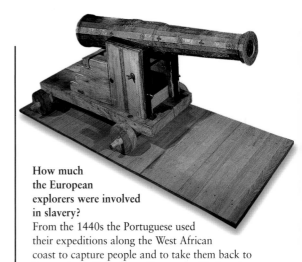

How much the European explorers were involved in slavery?
From the 1440s the Portuguese used their expeditions along the West African coast to capture people and to take them back to Portugal to sell as slaves. Europeans felt that slavery was justified because the people they had captured were not Christians. Once they became slaves, then they could become Christians. Africans began to fight back once they discovered why the Europeans were there. Portuguese traders soon realized that it would be easier to buy slaves from traders in the Benin.

What the history of the ancient civilizations was before the explorers "discovered" them?
We know very little about the lives of the Aztecs and Incas because the Spaniards destroyed everything that they found. Beautiful gold objects were melted down into gold bars. Books and drawings were burnt as works of the devil. Most of the remains of Tenochtitlan were not discovered until the Mexicans began to build an underground railway system in Mexico City.

GLOSSARY

ally A person, group, or country that has joined with another for a particular purpose.

amputation The surgical removal of a limb or body part.

anesthetic A drug that causes temporary loss of sensation in the body.

architecture The act or process of designing buildings.

armada A large fleet of warships.

arrears An unpaid debt that is overdue.

astronomical Relating to the study of the universe beyond Earth.

baptism A Christian ceremony that signifies spiritual cleansing and rebirth.

botany The scientific study of plants and vegetation.

charter To lease or rent services and possessions; a document issued by an authority that grants an institution certain rights or privileges.

charting Navigational mapping of coastlines and seas so that sailors can find routes for purposes of trade and exploration.

circumnavigate To travel all the way around something by ship.

coat of arms The symbol of a family, country, or organization. It shows designs and figures on and around a shield.

colonization The extension of a nation's power by the establishment of settlements and trade in foreign lands.

commander A person who leads and controls.

commemorate To honor the memory of someone.

commission A committee set up to deal with and look at a certain issue.

commodity Something that can be bought or sold.

compendium A collection of things.

dead reckoning A way of estimating one's current position based on a known previous position, allowing for speed, distance and direction moved.

deck A platform built on a ship. There are often numerous decks within a ship.

delicacy Expensive food.

dissolution The process of breaking up and destroying something. The "Dissolution of the Monasteries" was a process undertaken by King Henry VIII between 1536 and 1540, which resulted in the disbanding of all monasteries, nunneries, and friaries, and the claiming of their income, wealth, and land for the king.

dysentery An inflammatory infection of the intestines resulting in severe diarrhea. Dysentery was a major cause of death on board ship.

Elizabethan Relating to the reign of Elizabeth I.

engraving An image printed by using an engraved surface.

epic On a grand scale.

equator The imaginary line running around the center of Earth from east to west, at an equal distant from the North and South Poles.

exile The condition of being sent away from one's country and not allowed to return as a punishment.

exploit To make full use of and gain from.

flagship The ship in a fleet that carries the commanding admiral.

fleet A group of navy ships under one command.

gentry People of good social position, specifically (in Great Britain) the class of people next below the nobility in position and birth.

Global Positioning System Satellite system that allows users to pinpoint their location.

homage Special honor or respect shown publicly.

incite To urge to action by stirring up emotions.

investor A person or company that puts money into use for the purpose of making more money.

junk A Chinese sailing ship.

latitude The imaginary parallel lines running east to west around Earth.

longitude The imaginary parallel lines running north to south around Earth.

lucrative Producing a lot of profit.

malaria A disease spread by the bite of a mosquito.

missionary A person who tries to convert native inhabitants to their own religious viewpoint. Missionaries often provide charitable services.

mortality The likelihood of death. The mortality rate is the rate of death in a certain number of people in a population.

mutiny A rebellion by members of a ship's crew to overthrow the captain.

Native A person born in a particular place or country, and living there.

navigator A person who charts, sets, and steers the course of a ship or aircraft.

observatory A building designed and equipped for looking at the stars and for watching astronomical events.

patronage The support, encouragement, and backing (often financial) of a person or people.

pelt The skin or hide of an animal.

pillage Rob a place using violence.

plague A disease that spread quickly and killed many people in former times.

plunder To steal from by force.

piracy Stealing whilst at sea; taking ships and possessions without the instruction of a sovereign or ruler.

pivot A rod or pin upon which another part rotates, swings, or moves back and forth.

privateers An armed ship owned and officered by private individuals holding a government commission and authorized for use in war.

Protestant A Christian who belongs to a church other than the Catholic Church or an Eastern Orthodox church.

purser The person on board a ship who is responsible for all things financial.

putrefaction The decomposition or breakdown of a dead creature.

reprisal An act of retaliation.

repute The opinion generally held of someone or something.

revolt An act of resistance by one group of people against another.

scurvy A disease caused by not having enough vitamin C in the diet.

Spanish Main The mainland coast of the Spanish Empire around the Caribbean area.

spoils Material goods or othr things gained by winning a victory.

strait A narrow sea-channel, joining two larger bodies of water.

sugar cane A tall fibrous grass like plant, that naturally contains high levels of sucrose, which is refined to produce sugar.

treasurer The officer of a club, business, or other organization who is responsible for taking care of the group's money.

tribute The tax system employed by the Aztecs to support their state. This was paid by all the regions under their control to finance building, military, nobility, and religion.

Tudor Relating to the English royal family that held the throne from Henry VII in 1485 until the death of Elizabeth I in 1603.

typhoid An illness caused by eating or drinking contaminated food or water.

FURTHER READING
& WEBSITES

BOOKS

Atlas of Exploration
Andrew Kerr and Francois Naude
(Dorling Kindersley Publications, 2008)

Dead Reckoning: A Pirate Voyage with Captain Drake
Laurie Lawlor
(Simon & Schuster Children's Publishing, 2005)

*Elizabeth I and the Spanish Armada
(Stories from History)*
Colin Hynson (School Speciality Publishing, 2006)

Explorer (Eyewitness)
Rupert Matthews
(Dorling Kindersley Publications, 2003)

Explorers (Usborne Book Of . . .)
Felicity Everett (Usborne, 2007)

Explorers of the South Pacific: A Thousand Years of Exploration, from the Polynesians to Captain Cook and Beyond
Daniel E. Harmon (Mason Crest Publishers, 2002)

Francis Drake and the Sea Rovers of the Spanish Main (Qeb Pirates)
John Malam (Black Rabbit Books, 2008)

History Pockets: Explorers of North America
Mike Graf (Evan-Moor Educational Publishers, 2003)

*New York Public Library Amazing Explorers:
A Book of Answers for Kids*
Brendan January (Wiley, 2001)

Polar Explorers for Kids: Historic Expeditions to the Arctic and Antarctic with 21 Activities
Maxine Snowden (Chicago Review Press, 2003)

Sir Francis Drake (Explorers Set 1)
Kristin Petrie (Checkerboard Books, 2004)

Sir Francis Drake (Groundbreakers)
Neil Champion (Heinemann Library, 2001)

*Sir Francis Drake: Slave Trader and Pirate
(Wicked History)*
Charles Nick (Franklin Watts, 2009)

The Look-It-Up Book of Explorers (Look-It-Up Books)
Elizabeth Cody Kimmel (Random House, 2004)

The World Made New: Why the Age of Exploration Happened and How It Changed the World
Marc Aronson (National Geographic, 2007)

Tools of Navigation: A Kid's Guide to the History and Science of Finding Your Way (Tools of Discovery)
Rachel Dickinson (Nomad Press, 2005)

You Are the Explorer
Nathan Aaseng (Oliver Press, 1999)

You Wouldn't Want to Explore With Sir Francis Drake!: A Pirate You'd Rather Not Know
David Stewart (Children's Press (CT), 2005)

WEBSITES

http://academickids.com/encyclopedia/index.php/Francis_Drake
An encyclopedic biography of Sir Francis Drake with great cross-referencing to subjects related to his voyages.

www.bbc.co.uk/history/historic_figures/drake_francis.shtml
This BBC site has information on Sir Francis Drake and other Elizabethan explorers.

www.channel4.com/history/microsites/H/history/pirates/piratesdrake.html
A Channel 4 site that has information on Sir Francis Drake and the Spanish Armada.

www.kidskonnect.com/subject-index/16-history/265-explorers.html
A gateway to sites about the different explorers.

www.nmm.ac.uk/drake
The National Maritime Museum, London, site with a biography and details about Sir Francis Drake's voyages.

www.goldenhind.co.uk/education/index.html
The Education Center of the Golden Hind replica ship that is based in Devon, England. It provides useful information on Sir Francis Drake and Elizabethan exploration, including health, life on board, navigational instruments, and food.

www.lancsngfl.ac.uk/curriculum/history/index.php?category_id=22
An interactive introduction to the topic of Tudor exploration.

INDEX

ACKNOWLEDGMENTS

Consultant Editor: Pieter van der Merwe, National Maritime Museum.
We would also like to thank: Graham Rich, Peter Done, and Elizabeth Wiggans
for their assistance, and David Hobbs for his map of the world.
Picture research by Image Select.

NOTE TO READERS